117267

D1586685

Working Hours and Holidays

ok

Working Hours and Holidays

An employer's essential guide to the Working Time Regulations

LYNDA MACDONALD

www.hr-expert.com

FINANCIAL TIMES
Prentice Hall

London	New York	San Francisco	Toronto	Sydney
Tokyo	Singapore	Hong Kong	Cape Town	Madrid
Paris	Milan	Munich	Amsterdam	

PEARSON EDUCATION LIMITED

Head Office:
Edinburgh Gate
Harlow CM20 2JE
Tel: +44 (0) 1279 623623
Fax: +44 (0) 1279 431059

London Office:
128 Long Acre, London WC2E 9AN
Tel: +44 (0)171 447 2000
Fax: +44 (0)171 447 5771
Website: www.hr-expert.com

First published in Great Britain 2000

© Pearson Education Limited 2000

ISBN 0 273 64566 8

British Library Cataloguing in Publication Data
A CIP catalogue record for this book can be obtained from the British Library.

Transferred to digital print on demand, 2005

Printed & bound by Antony Rowe Ltd, Eastbourne

The publishers' policy is to use paper manufactured from sustainable forests.

About the author

Lynda A.C. Macdonald is a self-employed, freelance management trainer, employment law specialist and writer. For 15 years, prior to setting up her own consultancy business, she gained substantial practical experience of employee relations, recruitment and selection, dismissal procedures, employment law and other aspects of human resource management through working in industry. With this solid background in human resource management, she successfully established and currently runs her own business in management training and employment law/ human resource management consultancy. She is also appointed as a panel member of the Employment Tribunal service in Aberdeen, where she lives.

Lynda is a university graduate in language and a Fellow of the Institute of Personnel and Development, and also has an LLM degree in employment law and practice.

She first established herself as a business author in 1995 with the publication of a book on the subject of employment law/rights. More recently, she compiled a comprehensive loose-leaf manual on discrimination in the workplace embracing a wide range of employment law. The manual was published by a major publisher. She has subsequently written detailed text for Pearson Education on the subjects of termination of employment, discrimination, family-friendly policies and employee rights, including rights concerning working time and holidays.

Lynda can be contacted at:

1 Whitelands Road

Newtonhill

Aberdeen

AB39 3TR

Tel/fax: 01569 730277

e-mail: lyndamacdonald@clara.co.uk

Contents

Part I

The Working Time Regulations – background and scope   1

Part II

Working Hours   10

Part III

Part IV

Administration and Contracting out   53

Executive summary

- The Working Time Directive was implemented in the UK (by means of the *Working Time Regulations 1998*) on 1 October 1998. The Directive lays down restrictions with regard to working hours, compulsory rest periods and night working, and provides for minimum holiday entitlements (see: *Chapter 1*).

- There are certain exceptions and permitted derogations from some of the terms of the Regulations. Junior doctors, army and police officers, transport workers, sea fishing workers and others who work at sea are completely excluded (*Reg 18*) (see: *Chapter 2*).

- In accordance with the Regulations, employers are not permitted to compel employees to work longer than 48 hours per week, although employees may volunteer to work longer hours if they wish (see: *Chapter 3*).

- The Regulations prescribe a compulsory daily rest period of at least 11 consecutive hours, a weekly rest period of at least 24 hours, and a maximum night shift of 8 hours. These provisions apply to most workers (see: *Chapters 4 and 6*).

- Where an employee's working day exceeds 6 hours, they must be granted a rest break during the day (*Reg 12*). The length of this rest break will normally be a minimum of 20 minutes (see: *Chapter 4*).

- A requirement for an employee to work excessive or unreasonable hours could place the employer in breach of the common law duty to take reasonable care of the employee's health and safety (see: *Chapter 5*).

- Strict limitations are in place regarding the hours of work of children and young people (see: *Chapter 5*).

- The Regulations lay down a maximum average night shift of 8 hours, with 8 hours being the absolute maximum (i.e. no averaging) where the employee's work is hazardous, or involves physical or mental strain (see: *Chapter 6*).

- Employees are entitled to receive (within 2 months of commencing work) a written statement setting out the key terms and conditions of their employment. This statement must include working hours and holiday entitlement (*Employment Rights Act 1996 s 1(1)*) (see: *Chapters 7 and 10*).

- It is advisable for employers to examine their working practices with regard to working hours and overtime to ensure that their requirements do not place women at a disadvantage (see: *Chapter 7*).

- Employers may only alter employees' working hours if there is a flexibility clause in the contract of employment entitling them to do so, or if the employee has expressly agreed to the change (see: *Chapter 8*).

- Under the Regulations, all workers are entitled in law to 4 weeks' paid annual leave. No cash substitutes are allowed in lieu of holidays not taken, except on termination of employment (see: *Chapter 9*).

- There is no general right in law for employees to be granted time off on public holidays, nor to be paid at an enhanced rate of pay if the holiday is worked (see: *Chapter 10*).

- There are a number of provisions of the Regulations which can be modified by setting up an agreement between the employer and either trade union representatives or employee-elected representatives. The practical effect of this is that employers may modify the way in which the Regulations apply to them in certain defined areas (see: *Chapter 11*).

- The employer is obliged in law to keep certain records of employees' working hours, including night working. These must be made available for inspection by the Health and Safety Executive (see: *Chapter 12*).

- The records which employers must keep must include details of any relevant agreements entered into between the employer and the workforce and details of each worker who has signed an individual written agreement to work in excess of an average of 48 hours per week (see: *Chapter 12*).

- The Regulations are subject to a variety of enforcement measures including a right for workers to complain to an employment tribunal if their rights have been breached, criminal sanctions, enforcement by the Health and Safety Executive and potential claims by workers for breach of contract (see: *Chapter 12*).

- Irrespective of length of service, employees can complain to an employment tribunal if they are denied any of their rights under the Regulations. They also have the right not to be dismissed or subjected to a detriment for asserting their rights (see: *Chapter 12*).

- Measures to extend the terms of working hours legislation to those who are excluded from the scope of the Working Time Directive have been agreed in Europe. This will, in time, affect transport workers, sea fishermen, offshore workers and junior doctors (see: *Chapter 13*).

Table of cases

Table of statutes

List of Regulations

Part I

The Working Time Regulations – background and scope

Background to the Working Time Regulations 1998

1.1 INTRODUCTION

Since the implementation of the *Working Time Regulations 1998* on 1 October 1998, employees have, for the first time, the right to limit their working hours, take prescribed minimum rest breaks and be granted paid annual leave. Those who work at nights also have specific rights. Over and above the statutory provisions, there is the matter of employees' contractual rights (both express and implied) which the employer must respect. This Briefing provides an explanation of the statutory and contractual provisions concerning working hours and holidays, including a full explanation of the provisions of the Regulations.

The Regulations emanate from the EU Working Time Directive of 1993. This Directive was a major piece of European legislation which compelled the UK government to pass national legislation to regulate employees' working hours, time off and holiday entitlements (*European Council Directive 93/04/EC*).

Like all Directives, the Working Time Directive imposed an obligation on the governments of EU member states to pass national legislation to enact it. The enacting legislation has to incorporate the core provisions of the Directive, but may or may not include certain permitted derogations (see: *Section 2.4*). The exact form of the enacting legislation, and the extent and detail of its provisions, are therefore left up to each country to determine.

This means that in effect the UK government had considerable scope to determine the extent of UK working time legislation, and various options as to whether to incorporate some or all of the permitted derogations.

The principal aim of the Working Time Directive was to impose minimum health and safety requirements for the organisation of working time. The main provisions contained within the Working Time Regulations 1998 concern:

- working hours (see: *Chapter 3*);
- rest breaks (see: *Chapter 4*);
- night working (see: *Chapter 6*); and
- holiday entitlements (see: *Chapter 9*).

1.2 THE WORKING TIME DIRECTIVE AND ITS IMPLEMENTATION INTO UK LAW

The Working Time Directive should have been implemented in the UK by 23 November 1996. The Conservative government of the time was opposed to the principles contained in the Directive, i.e. the imposition of limitations on employers as to their employees' working hours and the creation of statutory

rights for employees to rest periods and holiday entitlements. It was the Conservative government's view that working time was a social issue, and that the Directive should form part of the Social Chapter, from which the UK was at that time opted out.

The government mounted a challenge at the European Court of Justice in late 1996 and put forward its views that working time should be considered a social issue, but they lost their case. The Court upheld the view of the other European member states that working time was a health and safety measure, and not a social issue. Furthermore, because health and safety measures require only qualified majority voting (rather than unanimous voting), no single country could veto the Working Time Directive. Consequently the UK had no choice but to implement the provisions of the Directive.

It perhaps seems academic now that, if working time had been a social measure, it would have been subject to the opt-out from the Social Chapter. In any event, the Labour government which came to power in May 1997 took steps to opt in to the Social Chapter and adopt the Directives contained within it. The Working Time Regulations were finally implemented on 1 October 1998.

The Regulations which implemented the Working Time Directive also implemented certain provisions of the Young Workers Directive of 1994 (*European Council Directive 94/33/EC*).

The scope of the Working Time Regulations 1998

2.1 INTRODUCTION

The wording of the *Working Time Regulations 1998* leaves many issues unclear, and the likelihood is that many important aspects of interpretation will end up being determined by the courts and tribunals as individuals begin to challenge and enforce their rights.

The Regulations apply to all employers, regardless of size. Exceptions exist with regard to certain jobs, but no employer is exempt from the Regulations.

The Regulations do, however, exempt certain categories of worker completely from their scope (*Reg 18*, see: *Section 2.4*).

2.2 THE MEANING OF WORKER

The *Working Time Regulations 1998* use the term 'worker' which is wider in scope than just employee. The law therefore compels employers to apply the entitlements afforded by the Regulations to agency staff, temporary employees, homeworkers, casuals and freelances. The Regulations state that the definition of 'worker' includes anyone who works under:

- a contract of employment, or
- any other contract, whether express or implied and (if express) whether oral or in writing, whereby the individual undertakes to perform personally any work or services for another party whose status is not that of a client or customer of any profession or business carried on by the individual.

Thus most workers are covered by the Regulations with the exception of self-employed individuals who are genuinely in business on their own account and are working directly for a client or customer (*Reg 2*).

The Regulations apply to part-time workers as well as full-timers.

2.3 WHAT IS AND IS NOT WORKING TIME

The scope of working time is not entirely clear from the *Working Time Regulations 1998*. The Working Time Directive states that 'working time is defined as any period during which the worker is working, at the employer's disposal, and carrying out his activity or duties, in accordance with the national laws and/or practice'. The Regulations adopt a similar approach with the result that the only statutory guidance for employers is that time will be working time in the following circumstances (*Reg 2*):

1 The employee is working, available to the employer and carrying out their duties.

2 The employee is receiving relevant training.

3 The time is defined as working time in a relevant agreement.

There is nothing to indicate that working time must equate with time spent at the person's workplace. Conversely, if the person is not actually working, then time spent at the workplace will not count as working time unless it is otherwise agreed.

Time spent on a training course will count as working time whether it takes place during normal working hours or at some other time.

There are a number of issues which remain unclear as they are not dealt with in the Regulations. Table 2.1 provides guidance on whether an activity can be classed as falling within the scope of working time.

Table 2.1   Guidance on whether an activity is 'working time'

Activity	Working time	Activity	Working time
Employee on call at home	No	Employee called out to work during off-duty hours	Yes
Employee choosing to eat lunch at desk, but could take a break if they wished	No, even if lunch break is paid	Employee attending business lunch, or meeting over lunch break	Yes, irrespective of whether lunch break is paid
Travel from home to work	No	Travel on business to another workplace, e.g. travel to a business meeting in another city	Yes, irrespective of whether travel time falls within normal working hours
Employee taking work home out of choice	Probably no	Employee asked or expected to take work home in order (for example) to complete it by a deadline	Yes

Another issue which has not been addressed in the statute is whether time off work for statutory reasons (for example time off for public duties, time off for ante-natal care, etc.) is to be counted as working time.

2.4 <u>PERMITTED EXEMPTIONS</u>

The *Working Time Regulations 1998* contain certain permitted exemptions (or derogations) which allow for adjustments to the rules and hence, potentially, limit the extent of the Regulations' application. These cover workers excluded from the Regulations and workers who have autonomy over their own hours or whose work is unmeasured.

2.4.1 Workers excluded from the Regulations

The *Working Time Regulations 1998* completely exclude certain categories of workers from their scope (*Reg 18*). These are:

- doctors under training;
- specified service activities such as the armed forces, the police and specific jobs within the civil protection services (although ordinary civil servants are covered);
- transport workers engaged in air, rail, road, sea, inland waterway and lake transport activities, although aircrew, train, bus and truck drivers, and the crew of sea-going vessels in any event have their own hours regulations;
- sea fishermen/women;
- people performing other work at sea, which covers those working on ships, and extends to employees working on offshore oil and gas installations.

Measures to extend the provisions of the 1993 Working Time Directive have been agreed. When implemented, these will introduce further legislation on working hours for junior doctors, transport workers, sea fishing workers and offshore workers (see: *Chapter 13*). The view is that the existing provisions do not go far enough, and that workers excluded from the Directive should be given some protection and rights to limit their working hours and receive minimum rest breaks and holidays.

The new provisions will also clarify that non-mobile workers in the transport sector (for example clerical workers) are covered by the Working Time Directive.

2.4.2 Workers who have autonomy over their own hours or whose work is unmeasured

The Working Time Directive envisaged that workers who genuinely had autonomy over their own working time would not need regulations to protect them. Hence derogations from most of the provisions of the *Working Time Regulations 1998* may be applied to workers where, due to the specific characteristics of their work,

the length of their working time is not measured or predetermined, or where working time can be decided by the workers themselves (*Reg 20*). Potential examples of such workers are given in the Regulations as managing executives or other persons with autonomous decision-taking powers, family workers, and workers officiating at religious ceremonies in churches and religious communities. These, however, are only examples.

The scope of the term 'managing executive' has given rise to some doubt and uncertainty. The philosophy governing this exemption is that it covers those workers who genuinely have control over the number of hours they work to the extent that they can determine how many hours they work. Apart from some senior managers, this exemption could potentially apply to some sales executives, maintenance staff, and homeworkers whose working hours are not measured, or are predetermined by the worker rather than the employer.

It is important to note that this derogation does not apply to holiday entitlement. Consequently managing executives and other workers with autonomy will retain a statutory right to the minimum holiday entitlement imposed by the Regulations (4 weeks per annum) (see: *Chapter 9*).

The Government has recently changed the section of the Regulations which deals with unmeasured working time so that some of a worker's time may now be exempted from the normal rules. The 'managing executive' derogation now applies in part to workers who choose of their own volition to work additional hours beyond the portion of their working time which is pre-determined (for example the core hours specified in their contract of employment). This does not affect employees who are required by their employer to work additional hours, nor those who are paid for overtime, but instead affects only additional hours which are clearly worked on a voluntary basis. The sorts of workers likely to fall within this group are those who can determine when they start and finish work, have latitude to prioritise between tasks and can choose how much time to work on different activities (typically managers).

The effect of this change is that the additional hours which the employee chooses to work will be disregarded in respect of the 48-hour limit, thus removing the need for such workers to sign an opt-out or maintain records of the hours they work.

This amendment does not remove any workers affected by it from the right to limit the core hours they are obliged to work by the employer to a maximum average of 48 hours per week, nor from the entitlement to rest breaks and paid annual leave. Furthermore, the change does not affect those workers who currently fall within the 'unmeasured working time' derogation.

Part II

Working Hours

3

Working hours

3.1   INTRODUCTION

One of the most far-reaching provisions of the *Working Time Regulations 1998* is that there is a maximum average working week of 48 hours (including overtime) over a 'reference period' of 17 weeks (*Regs 4 and 5*).

Unless the employer specifies otherwise, this 17-week reference period will be a rolling period. This means that employers must ensure that employees do not work more than an average of 48 hours per week taken over any 17-week period.

Employers, may, however, agree to use defined periods of 17 weeks for the purpose of calculating employees' average working hours. In this case, each reference period will have a specified start and finish date, with the next reference period running consecutively with the last one. This may be useful where, due to the nature of the employer's business, there are known peaks in activity at certain times. There is a restriction on this provision for new employees (see: *Section 3.2*).

One of the exemptions from the provisions of the Regulations relating to rest periods and night working is that the averaging provision may extend over a longer reference period in certain circumstances (see: *Sections 4.5 and 6.7*). For certain categories of workers it can be 26 weeks rather than 17. There is also the option in certain circumstances for employers to set up a collective or workforce agreement providing for a 1-year reference period for averaging working time, providing there are objective or technical reasons for doing so.

Where a worker has more than one job, employers are required to take all reasonable steps to ensure that their working hours do not exceed an average of 48 in total. Employers should, therefore, put in place appropriate measures to ensure they are informed if their workers take up other employment, so that they may deal with the matter appropriately.

It is important to note that the statutory provisions concern actual working hours and not the number of hours specified in an individual's contract.

Sick leave, holidays and maternity leave must be excluded from the 48-hour averaging mechanism. This means that employers will not be permitted to regard a week during which an employee has been off sick (for example) as a nil-hours week and use it to offset weeks in which they have worked excessive hours.

3.2   LIMITS ON WORKING HOURS FOR NEW EMPLOYEES

One restriction on the calculation of average working hours is that, during the first 17 weeks of an individual's employment, the average working hours must be calculated over the period the person has actually worked. This means that it will

not be possible for an employee to exceed 48 hours in their first working week and, during the following weeks, the hours worked taken as an average over the number of weeks worked must at no time exceed 48 (*Reg 4(4)*). Example 3.1 illustrates this.

Example 3.1

A new employee works 46 hours during their first week of employment. In the second week, the individual cannot work more than 50 hours, because otherwise the average hours of the 2 weeks worked so far would exceed 48. If the person works 50 hours in the second week, the number of hours in the third week must consequently not exceed 48.

However, if during the first week of employment, the individual has worked 40 hours, it would in theory be permissible for them to work up to 56 hours in the second week. If, however, only 44 hours were worked in the second week, this would leave an option for the individual to work up to 60 hours in the third week, because in this example the average of the 3 weeks (40+44+60) is 48.

This limitation imposed on the hours of new employees may have a particular impact on employers who employ temporary workers to cover peaks in the workload or special short-term projects.

3.3 THE FACILITY FOR EMPLOYEES TO VOLUNTEER TO WORK LONGER HOURS

The *Working Time Regulations 1998* provide that, where an individual worker volunteers to work more than 48 hours in a particular week, the employer may permit the person to do so. The limitations on this derogation are set out below (*Reg 5*):

1 Any agreement for an individual to work more than an average of 48 hours per week must be in writing with that individual. It is not permissible to use a collective or workforce agreement to exclude a group of workers from the 48-hour limit (see: *Sections 11.2 and 11.3*).

2 Where an individual has agreed in writing to work more than an average of 48 hours per week, they may terminate the agreement at any time by giving notice. The notice period cannot be less than 7 days or more than 3 months as specified in the agreement.

3 The employer must keep up-to-date and accurate records of all workers who have opted out of the 48-hour limitation and any conditions on which they have agreed to opt out (see: *Chapter 12*).

The requirement for employers to maintain detailed records of the hours of every opted-out worker was abolished in December 1999 (*Working Time Regulations 1999 Reg 3*). However, the requirement to keep a record of which workers have signed an opt-out remains in force.

These opt-out arrangements are to be reviewed by the European Commission by November 2003. Since the UK is the only EU country to have taken advantage of the derogation permitting employees to opt out of the 48-hour maximum, it is possible that, after the year 2003, it will no longer be permissible for employees to volunteer to work more than an average of 48 hours per week.

Where an employee opts out of the 48-hour limitation, their opting-out notice would normally be of indefinite length. However, a worker may alternatively state a specific period to which their opt-out relates. Furthermore, workers who have opted out of the 48-hour limitation may opt back in again at any time. The 7-day notice period for opting back in to the 48-hour limit may be varied by an appropriate collective, workforce or relevant agreement up to a maximum of 3 months (see: *Sections 11.2, 11.3 and 11.4*).

It is important to note that this provision for voluntary agreement from the employee applies only to the maximum weekly hours provision, and not to rest periods or holiday entitlements. Employees are not permitted to volunteer to forego their daily or weekly rest period, nor to work through their annual leave entitlement.

The *Working Time Regulations 1998* also contain provisions preventing employers from subjecting workers to any detriment for refusing to sign such an opt out (*Employment Rights Act 1996 s 45(a)*).

4

Rest breaks

4.1 <u>INTRODUCTION</u>

There are a range of compulsory rest periods from which workers are entitled to benefit under the *Working Time Regulations 1998*. These are:

- rest break during the working day (see: *Section 4.2*);
- daily rest period (see: *Section 4.3*);
- weekly rest period (see: *Section 4.4*).

The right for employees to take rest periods is framed in the legislation as an entitlement rather than something which employers are compelled to force upon employees. This means that, whilst employers must not prevent employees from taking their rest periods, and must not penalise them for doing so, they need not stop an employee from working through a particular rest period if the employee chooses to do so. This must, however, be the employee's choice and not the employer's.

There is no provision in the Regulations that rest breaks should be paid, and payment is thus a matter for the employment contract to specify.

4.2 <u>REST BREAK DURING THE WORKING DAY</u>

If an individual's working day exceeds 6 hours, there must be a compulsory rest break during the day of at least 20 minutes (*Reg 12*). Workers are entitled, if they wish, to leave their workplace during this rest break.

Employers may, however, through workforce or collective agreements, modify or exclude the break (*Reg 23(a)*, see: *Sections 11.2 and 11.3*).

This means that all workers who work at least 6 hours per day have to be permitted to take a single 20-minute break from work (for example, a lunch break) rather than simply working through the whole day with (for example) a coffee and sandwich at their desk.

4.3 <u>DAILY REST PERIOD</u>

It is compulsory to grant workers a daily rest period of at least 11 consecutive hours every 24 hours (*Reg 10*). This may be restrictive for employers, as no averaging is permitted in the application of this provision.

This provision will affect employers whose current working practices occasionally demand that an employee works late into the evening with an early start at work the following day. In particular it may have a profound effect on

employees who are required to be on call, and who are in fact called out during hours that would normally constitute part of their daily rest period. This is because the *Working Time Regulations 1998* state that the daily rest period must be 11 consecutive hours (rather than 11 hours punctuated with periods of working time in between). The only exceptions are certain categories of worker exempted completely from the Regulations, and workers whose work cannot be predetermined (*Regs 19–21*, see: *Section 2.4*). There is provision for modification or exclusion by collective or workforce agreement (*Reg 23(a)*, see: *Section 4.5*).

4.4 WEEKLY REST PERIOD

The *Working Time Regulations 1998* impose a compulsory weekly rest period of at least 24 hours (uninterrupted), which may be averaged out over 2 weeks (*Reg 11*). The 2-week reference period, according to the Regulations, will start at midnight on a Sunday unless a relevant agreement provides otherwise (see: *Section 11.4*). It was suggested in the Regulations that this period should be added to the daily (11-hour) rest period wherever possible, giving employees a weekly continuous break of at least 35 hours.

This means that it will be feasible for an employee to work for up to 12 days without a day off, provided they are subsequently permitted to take at least 2 complete days off, over and above the usual daily rest breaks.

4.5 POSSIBLE EXEMPTIONS FROM THE REST PERIOD PROVISIONS

Certain categories of workers may be exempted from the provisions relating to minimum rest periods (and also length of night work) (*Reg 21*, see: *Section 6.7*). It is important to note, however, that this derogation does not affect the right for workers to limit their hours to a maximum average of 48 per week, i.e. the derogation excludes working hours. It does, however, provide employers with some flexibility as regards the timing of rest periods for certain categories of workers.

Where, as a result of this derogation, workers do not take the laid-down minimum rest periods, they must be given equivalent periods of compensatory rest. Thus the derogation simply permits employers flexibility in organising rest periods, and does not allow them to deny employees the right to take rest periods altogether.

The periods of time over which average hours may be calculated (the reference period) may be adjusted to 26 weeks for these categories of worker. Additionally a further derogation may be made by means of a collective or workforce agreement to vary the reference period so that it is extended to 52 weeks where justified by objective or technical reasons concerning the organisation of work (*Reg 23(b)*). This could be very important for certain employers who operate a system of annualised hours.

The list of workers potentially covered by the derogation relating to minimum rest periods is fairly broad, and covers the following (*Reg 21*):

1 Workers who have to travel some distance to get to work or who travel extensively between different workplaces. A typical example would be a construction worker who, during the week, works at a construction site distant from their home.

2 Security and surveillance workers where there is a requirement for a continuous presence throughout the day and night. This could include security guards, caretakers, etc.

3 Workers involved in a business where 24-hour continuity of service/production is required. This is based on a provision contained within the Working Time Directive which states that this derogation could apply whenever work cannot be interrupted on technical grounds. The *Working Time Regulations 1998* give a number of examples of such workers, including those working in:

   ■ reception, treatment or care activities in hospitals, residential institutions and prisons;

   ■ docks and airports;

   ■ press, radio, television and film production;

   ■ postal and telecommunications services;

   ■ civil protection services, such as ambulance and fire services, air and sea rescue and aircraft control;

   ■ gas, water and electricity production, transmission and distribution;

   ■ household refuse collection and incineration;

   ■ research and development activities;

   ■ agriculture.

4 Workers involved in peak periods of work, e.g. work with seasonal highs, such as work in agriculture, tourism and postal work.

5 Workers affected by unusual and unforeseeable circumstances, or where there has been an accident.

There are also special rules relating to shift changes which exclude daily and weekly rest periods in respect of the following workers (*Reg 22*):

1   Shift workers during the changeover from day to night shift (or vice versa) if they are unable on that occasion to take their daily and/or weekly rest period between the end of one shift and the start of the next one.

2   Workers who work split shifts, i.e. work split up over the day.

It is vital to bear in mind that, whenever a rest period is not taken, the employer must grant an equivalent period of compensatory rest, and that the obligation to restrict the average maximum working week to 48 hours still exists for these categories of worker.

5

Working hours and health and safety

5.1 INTRODUCTION

There is a general duty imposed on employers to ensure, so far as is reasonably practicable, the health, safety and welfare at work of all employees (*Health & Safety at Work Act 1974 s 2(1)*). This statement is capable of being interpreted so as to mean that employers are prevented from requiring employees to work excessive hours or unsuitable shift patterns, if the hours or shift patterns are likely to lead to ill-health or accidents.

5.2 HEALTH AND SAFETY UNDER THE WORKING TIME DIRECTIVE

The Working Time Directive, which is the source of the UK's *Working Time Regulations 1998*, was passed into legislation as a health and safety measure with the aim of imposing minimum health and safety requirements for the organisation of working time.

Apart from the main provisions covering working hours, rest breaks, night working and minimum holiday entitlements, the Regulations impose requirements on employers to alleviate the effects of monotonous work and work performed at a predetermined work rate. Although the Regulations do not specify what steps employers should take to achieve this, they do state that employers must ensure that workers are given 'adequate rest breaks' (*Reg 11*). This has been interpreted as meaning that employers should give workers who perform monotonous work more frequent breaks from work.

5.3 BREACH OF THE DUTY OF CARE

In parallel with the provisions of the *Health and Safety at Work Act 1974*, employers have a duty in common law to take reasonable care for the health and safety of their employees as part of the law of negligence. If an employee's physical or mental health has been damaged as a result of the employer's working practices, they may take a claim for personal injury to court.

Employers should therefore examine their working hours requirements to ensure that they do not make unreasonable demands on their employees, such that damage to health may occur.

In the case of *Johnstone v Bloomsbury Health Authority [1991]*, which was brought to court on account of an alleged breach of the implied contractual duty to take care of the employee's safety, the Court of Appeal said (in a minority view):

"The employers could not lawfully require the plaintiff hospital doctor to work so much overtime in any week as it was reasonably foreseeable would damage his health, notwithstanding the express terms of his contract of employment which required him to work 40 hours and to be available for a further 48 hours of overtime on average each week."

5.4 EMPLOYMENT OF CHILDREN AND YOUNG PERSONS

Restrictions on working hours are in place for young people under the age of 16 years (termed for this purpose as 'children'). The *Children Act 1972* lays down that the minimum age at which a child may be employed is 13. Other restrictions are that a child may not be employed:

- before the end of school hours on any day on which the child is required to attend school;

- before 7.00 a.m. or after 7.00 p.m. on any day;

- for more than 2 hours on any day on which the child is required to attend school;

- for more than 2 hours on any Sunday.

In any case, where an employer wishes to employ a child under 16 years of age, a permit must be obtained from the local education authority. Local authorities have the power to require employers to provide them with information about the employment of children. A special licence is also required if a child is to be allowed to take part in an entertainment performance, for example in a theatre.

Additionally, in 1998 new Regulations for the protection of children at work came into force (*Children (Protection at Work) Regulations 1998 SI 1998/276*). These Regulations represent part of the implementation of the EU Young Workers Directive. They introduced the following:

1 A right for children to have a 2-week break from work during the school holidays.

2 A requirement for local authorities to update their bye-laws and create a list of jobs which 13 year olds may do. Thereafter children aged 13 are only permitted to do a job if it is on the list.

3 Controls on the employment of children in performances were extended to include children employed in sport and advertising, including modelling work.

Restrictions on the hours of work of young persons aged 16 and 17 are now in the *Working Time Regulations 1998*. These provide:

- a daily rest period of 12 consecutive hours;
- a weekly rest period of 2 days out of every 7 days;
- a rest break of at least 30 minutes after 4½ hours' work;
- a free health assessment prior to any night work assignment, and checks at regular intervals thereafter.

There are also a number of other health and safety provisions in place affecting the employment of young persons (*Health and Safety (Young Persons) Regulations 1997*). Employers must carry out risk assessments before a young person under 18 commences employment and, where children under 16 are involved, must also inform their parents of any risks that have been identified. Certain work activities are banned.

6

Night working

6.1   INTRODUCTION

The *Working Time Regulations 1998*, as a health and safety measure, have imposed a number of limitations on night working. The Regulations impose a requirement that employees' normal night shifts must not be more than 8 hours per night, averaged over a reference period of 17 weeks. This rule, in contrast to the rule regarding the weekly limit of 48 working hours, applies to an employee's normal night hours, rather than to their actual working hours. Night workers remain free, therefore, to agree to work voluntary overtime (but not contractual overtime imposed as a requirement by the employer).

6.2   THE DEFINITION OF NIGHT TIME

The *Working Time Regulations 1998* state that night time is a period of not less than 7 hours, and must at least cover the period spanning 12 midnight to 5.00 a.m. (*Reg 2*). The specific 7-hour period can be determined by a workforce or collective agreement (see: *Sections 11.2 and 11.3*). If no workforce or collective agreement is in place which covers this issue, then night time must be interpreted as the period running from 11.00 p.m. until 6.00 a.m. (*Reg 2*).

6.3   WORKERS REGARDED AS NIGHT WORKERS

A night worker is someone who works at least 3 hours during night time 'as a normal course'. 'Normal course' is defined so that someone who works at least 3 hours during night time on the majority of their working days will be classed as a night worker. Example 6.1 illustrates this.

Example 6.1

> An employee who works in a bar from 8.00 p.m. until 2.00 a.m. on 3 nights and from 4 p.m. to 10 p.m. on 2 nights a week is brought into the definition of night worker because in this example 3 hours of the employee's working time on 3 out of the 5 working days fall within the core period of night time.

A worker may also be regarded as a night worker if they work 'a certain proportion of his or her annual working time' during night time.

It is clear that individuals may be regarded as night workers even if they divide their time between day and night working. This will be so where a material proportion of the person's working time is spent on night working. In a case in

Northern Ireland (*R v Attorney General for Northern Ireland ex parte Burns, High Court 15.03.99*), the High Court ruled that a worker who spent 1 week of each 3-week cycle working at least 3 hours during the night was a night worker.

6.4   RESTRICTIONS ON NIGHT WORKERS

Employers who operate shift systems are advised to review those systems as an immediate priority, and to review whether any changes are required as a result of the introduction of the *Working Time Regulations 1998*.

Where employees' normal or contractual night hours exceed an average of 8 hours per night, the employer will have to alter the shift pattern so as to comply with the Regulations. Where change is necessary, time should be allowed for proper consultation and discussion of the most acceptable alternatives. Example 6.2 illustrates this.

Example 6.2

An employer operates a shift system which involves a night shift commencing at 8.00 p.m. and finishing at 6.00 a.m. Employees on night shift usually work 4 nights per week, totalling 40 hours. This pattern will fall within the limitations prescribed by the Regulations so long as the employees' contracts provide for them to work only 4 nights per week. This is because the night-working provisions relate to normal or contractual night hours, unlike the provisions governing the 48-hour week, which relate to actual hours worked. Thus the averaging mechanism ensures that the employer's shift system remains within the scope of the law.

6.5   RESTRICTIONS ON NIGHT WORKERS WHO PERFORM HAZARDOUS WORK

The *Working Time Regulations 1998* provide for an absolute 8-hour maximum on night working if the employee's work involves special hazards or if it involves heavy physical or mental strain. This means that no averaging will be allowed in these circumstances.

It is important to note also that, with regard to the hours of workers involved in hazardous work, it is actual working hours which are limited, and not normal or contractual hours.

Night work, under the Regulations, is regarded as involving special hazards or heavy physical or mental strain if either:

26

■ a workforce or collective agreement has identified it as such, or

■ a risk assessment carried out by the employer has classified the work as involving significant risk to the health and safety of the workers (*Management of Health and Safety at Work Regulations 1992 Reg 3*).

Even with this clarification, 'mental strain' may be difficult to pin down although 'physical strain' may not pose too great a problem.

6.6 <u>WORKERS' RIGHTS TO FREE HEALTH CHECKS</u>

Workers who are classed as night workers are entitled to a free health assessment before being assigned to night work, and subsequently at regular intervals. The purpose of the health assessments is to ensure that night workers are fit to perform night work. If a night worker is found to be suffering from health problems connected with the fact that they work at night, they will have the right to be transferred as soon as possible to day work. There are no derogations from this provision.

6.7 <u>POSSIBLE EXEMPTIONS FROM THE NIGHT-WORKING PROVISIONS</u>

Certain categories of workers may be exempted from the provisions relating to length of night work (and also minimum rest periods) (*Reg 21*, see *Section 4.5*). It is important to note, however, that this derogation does not affect the right for workers to limit their hours to a maximum average of 48 per week – i.e. the derogation excludes working hours. It does, however, provide employers with some flexibility as regards the scheduling of night work for certain categories of workers.

The periods of time over which average hours may be calculated (the reference period) may be adjusted to 26 weeks for these categories of worker. Additionally, a further derogation may be made by means of a collective or workforce agreement to vary the reference period so that it is extended to 52 weeks where justified by objective or technical reasons concerning the organisation of work (*Reg 23(b)*, see *Sections 11.2 and 11.3*). This could be very important for certain employers who operate a system of annualised hours.

The list of workers potentially covered by the derogation relating to length of night work is fairly broad, and covers the following:

1 Workers who have to travel some distance to get to work or who travel extensively between different workplaces. A typical example would be a construction worker who, during the week, works at a construction site distant from their home.

2 Security and surveillance workers where there is a requirement for a continuous presence throughout the day and night. This would include security guards, caretakers, etc.

3 Workers involved in a business where 24-hour continuity of service/production is required. This is based on a provision contained within the Working Time Directive which states that this derogation could apply whenever work cannot be interrupted on technical grounds. The *Working Time Regulations 1998* give a number of examples of such workers, including those working in:

- reception, treatment or care activities in hospitals, residential institutions and prisons;
- docks and airports;
- press, radio, television and film production;
- postal and telecommunications services;
- civil protection services, such as ambulance and fire services, air and sea rescue, and aircraft control;
- gas, water and electricity production, transmission and distribution;
- household refuse collection and incineration;
- research and development activities;
- agriculture.

4 Workers involved in peak periods of work, e.g. work with seasonal highs, such as work in agriculture, tourism and postal work.

5 Workers affected by unusual and unforeseeable circumstances, or where there has been an accident (*Reg 21*).

7

Working hours and contracts of employment

7.1 <u>INTRODUCTION</u>

Prior to the introduction of the provisions contained within the *Working Time Regulations 1998*, there were no restrictions on employers with regard to employees' working hours (except for drivers of goods vehicles and public service vehicles, and airline pilots). Even with the introduction of the Regulations, employers may, so long as they comply with the provisions of the Regulations, determine what employees' working hours should be by means of the contract of employment.

7.2 <u>EMPLOYEE'S RIGHT TO A WRITTEN STATEMENT DETAILING THEIR WORKING HOURS</u>

There is a duty on employers to provide employees with a written statement outlining the key terms and conditions of their employment (*Employment Rights Act 1996 s 1(1)*). This right accrues to all employees who continue in employment for at least 1 month; thus temporary staff engaged on a contract of less than 1 month are excluded. The written statement must be provided to employees within 2 months of commencing work (*Employment Rights Act 1996 s 1(2)*). Part-time employees have the same right in this respect as full-time staff.

The written statement is in effect a statement setting out the key terms which govern the employment relationship. It forms a major part of the employee's contract of employment, although the contract may include other terms and rules which are not contained in the statement, but appear elsewhere (for example, in an employee handbook).

The written statement must include (among other items) a statement outlining the employee's normal working hours (*Employment Rights Act 1996 s 1(4)(c)*). The statement should also include any rules as to hours of work, overtime requirements and any flexibility which is required. The key aim is to provide the employee with a clear statement on the hours which they are contractually required to work, and the need for flexibility if this is required as part of the working arrangements.

There is no requirement for the employer to state specific hours of work in the written statement (for example 9.00 a.m. to 5.00 p.m. from Monday to Friday with 1 hour off for lunch each day), although employers may do this if they wish. If the employer wishes an employee to work variable hours, then the written statement can specify this. Similarly, if the job requires the employee to be available to work additional hours beyond the stated normal working hours, then a condition to this effect may be included within the written statement. The written

statement may even say that the employee is required to work any reasonable number of hours according to the needs of the job. Model flexibility clauses are available (see: *Section 8.4*).

In any event, employers should ensure that their requirements as to hours of work are set out precisely in the contract of employment. The following issues should be covered, depending on the relevant working patterns:

1 Normal working hours and total number of hours to be worked during the week.

2 Timing and duration of lunch breaks. Employees can be required to take lunch breaks at a fixed time, or within a set period (for example, 1 hour between 12.00 noon and 2 p.m.).

3 Timing and duration of any other breaks.

4 Overtime requirements and arrangements, including whether the employee will be paid for any overtime worked.

5 Precise terms for any flexible working arrangements. These should include, for example, the minimum number of hours which have to be worked, 'core' hours when the employee has to attend for work, and time-recording procedures. Normally the employer should reserve the right to adapt or stop the flexible arrangement if this is necessary for operational reasons.

6 Details of shift patterns, including any shift allowance. Employers should reserve the right to alter shift patterns if necessary for operational reasons.

7.3 OVERTIME REQUIREMENTS

Employers should clearly specify any terms and conditions relating to overtime in the contract of employment. Employers should consider including provisions on the following issues:

- whether overtime is to be paid or unpaid;
- what rates of pay will apply during overtime hours;
- whether employees will only be required to work overtime if they agree to do so, or whether overtime is to be dictated by the needs of the business;
- special rules and procedures which will apply (e.g. that employees must obtain written authorisation from management before working overtime).

Employers should note the particular need to treat part-time employees reasonably in relation to overtime provisions. It will not normally be appropriate to require part-timers to work overtime without their express consent, or to require them to work additional hours without paying overtime.

7.4 WHY A REQUIREMENT FOR EXTENSIVE OVERTIME/WEEKEND WORKING/NIGHT WORKING MIGHT DISCRIMINATE AGAINST WOMEN

Sex discrimination law has developed extensively over the past few years and employers need to take care to ensure that their working practices do not inadvertently discriminate against women (or men).

Indirect sex discrimination occurs where a practice or policy adversely affects one sex more than the other, and will be unlawful unless the employer can show that it is justifiable (*Sex Discrimination Act 1975 s 1(1)(b)*).

Indirect discrimination occurs when the following circumstances exist (*Sex Discrimination Act 1975 s 1(1)(b)*):

- the employer imposes a requirement or condition on all employees, and

- because of the nature of the requirement, a considerably smaller proportion of women than men (or men than women) can comply with it, and

- the requirement or condition is to an employee's detriment because they cannot comply with it, and

- the employer is unable to show that the requirement or condition is justifiable on objective grounds and irrespective of sex.

It has been generally accepted by the courts that women are less able to comply with a requirement to work long hours because in general more family responsibilities fall to women than to men. Thus hours requirements which involve irregular shiftwork, compulsory weekend working, occasional or regular night work or excessive overtime could place a female employee at a disadvantage if she was unable to comply with the hours required of her owing to domestic or child-minding responsibilities.

Ultimately the key question is whether the hours of work required of an employee can be justified. To establish justification, the hours of work must represent a real business need, and be appropriate and necessary for the achievement of that need. Otherwise it is possible that a woman could succeed in a case of indirect sex discrimination if she is required to work, for example, excessive overtime in the evenings or at weekends, and suffers a detriment for not being able to comply. But if the employer can objectively justify the need for the hours of work required of the employee, there will be no unlawful sex discrimination.

An example of sex discrimination as a result of a change of hours occurred in a case where an employee who was a single mother was, because of her child-care

responsibilities, unable to comply with a new shift system introduced by her employer (*London Underground Ltd v Edwards [1997]*). Despite being the only employee in this position, she succeeded in a case of unlawful sex discrimination. The Court of Appeal held that the employer could not justify insisting that she should work the new shift pattern. The key principle for employers is that they should be certain that any hours requirement imposed on employees, both individually and collectively, can be objectively justified based on the needs of the business.

It is advisable for employers to review their hours requirements from time to time, and to examine whether the requirements which they are imposing on their employees can in fact be justified on objective job-based grounds.

Employer's right to alter working hours/shifts

8.1 INTRODUCTION

If an employer wishes to alter the working hours or shift patterns of an employee or group of employees, they can only do this lawfully in the following circumstances:

■ if there is a flexibility clause in the employee's contract entitling the employer to change the employee's hours (the limits in the clause must be complied with), or

■ if the employee expressly agrees to the change.

A model flexibility clause relating to the alteration of shift patterns is available (see: *Section 8.4*).

8.2 POSSIBLE CONSEQUENCES OF IMPOSING A CHANGE OF HOURS WITHOUT THE EMPLOYEE'S AGREEMENT

If the employer attempts to force an employee to work different or longer hours without agreement, the employee may react in one of a number of ways:

1 The employee may simply refuse to work under the new terms. Contractually they would be entitled to refuse. If the employer dismisses the employee for refusing in these circumstances, this would in all probability give the employee a claim for wrongful dismissal and unfair dismissal (unless there was a suitable flexibility clause in the contract).

2 If the employee works under the new contract without protest, acceptance of the new terms will, after a reasonable period of time, be implied, even although no written agreement has been obtained. There is no time frame laid down in law for this implied agreement to take effect. However, in practice, a few weeks would be sufficient. Hence, by working the new hours and doing nothing to indicate an objection to the imposed changes, the employee effectively consents to the change.

3 The employee may work under the new terms under protest, i.e. may (while actually working the new hours) write to the employer stating that they have not agreed to work the new hours and object to their imposition. By adopting this course of action, the employee effectively buys more time to decide on whether to take any legal action against the employer under 4 and 5 below.

4 The employee may resign and claim constructive dismissal based on the argument that the employer has breached the terms of the contract of

employment by enforcing a change of hours. For this to succeed, the breach of contract must be fundamental (i.e. not a trivial or minor change), and the employee must act fairly quickly. A minimum service period of 1 year is required for eligibility to claim unfair dismissal.

5 Less drastically, the employee may sue for breach of contract. This might result in an injunction to stop the employer proceeding with the alteration of hours, or at least money damages in compensation, without the employee giving up their job.

Employers may also wish to consider the impact on employee morale of forcing unwelcome changes on employees. Low morale can lead to industrial relations problems, high absence levels, employee stress, low productivity and a host of other potential problems for the employer.

8.3 HOW TO ALTER AN EMPLOYEE'S HOURS OF WORK LAWFULLY

Obviously employers need to alter terms of employment from time to time in order to cope with changes in their business activities, but, where no flexibility clause exists in the contracts to authorise changes to working hours, then fair procedures must be observed before any change can be properly introduced.

Provided that the employer has sound business reasons for wishing to impose changes to working hours, it is possible to achieve the desired changes by going though a process of consultation followed by an invitation to employees to accept the new terms. If, following consultation, employees still refuse to agree to the proposed changes, then the employer may proceed by terminating existing contracts of employment (with notice) and offering re-engagement on the new terms. See *Appendix C1* for a procedure detailing how to proceed with this.

8.4 FLEXIBILITY CLAUSES

Employers can avoid the potential pitfalls and difficulties that occur in the event of a need to alter hours of work by ensuring that all employees have a suitably worded flexibility clause in their contracts of employment.

It is important to note that the flexibility clause must cover the specific type of change that the employer wishes to introduce. Usually there are two key issues:

- the number of working hours per week, and
- the timing of working, e.g. shift working and which days of the week are worked.

The employer should take care to anticipate what type of flexibility is required from employees and ensure that a clearly drafted clause covering the type of flexibility required is written into employees' contracts of employment at the outset of employment. This is because a clause entitling the employer to move an employee from day to night shift would not entitle them to lengthen or shorten the employee's working hours or reduce pay. Similarly a clause entitling the employer to require an employee to work at weekends would not provide authority to shorten working hours.

There is also the very important issue of whether pay is to be altered in the event of a change to the employee's contractual working hours or shift pattern. The Employment Appeal Tribunal (EAT) has ruled that a reduction in an employee's pay following a move to a different shift pattern, in a situation where the employer was contractually entitled to alter the employee's shift pattern, was not an unlawful deduction from wages (*Hussman Manufacturing v Weir (1998) IRLR 258*). Nevertheless, it is safer for employers to ensure that there is a separate statement in the contract which explicitly authorises alterations to pay in the event of a change of hours or shifts.

Model flexibility clauses are set out below.

> It is a condition of your employment that you are available to work any reasonable number of hours which your job requires in order to fulfil your duties and responsibilities. This requirement is subject to the limitations imposed by statute.

> Normal office hours are from 09.00–16.30 hours from Monday to Friday, but you may be asked to work longer days and/or to be available to work at weekends according to organisational requirements. It is a condition of your employment that you agree to work additional hours when reasonably asked to do so.

> You will not receive any additional pay for hours worked over and above normal office hours.

> The company operates a flexible shift pattern covering 24 hours per day, 7 days per week. Your normal shift hours are from 08.00 a.m. to 4.00 p.m. 5 days per week, working from Tuesday to Saturday inclusive.
>
> The company reserves the right to alter your shift pattern according to the needs of the business. You may be asked to move to another shift (including night shift working), or to work on different days of the week, and it is a condition of your employment that you agree to such changes if requested. Such moves may be on a permanent or temporary basis.

Part III

Holidays

Statutory holiday entitlements

9.1 INTRODUCTION

The *Working Time Regulations 1998* impose a compulsory period of paid annual leave of 4 weeks for all workers. The initial period of statutory leave was 3 weeks per annum, but this was increased to 4 weeks as from 23 November 1999 (see: *Section 9.3*).

Part-time workers are entitled to the appropriate pro-rata portion of statutory annual leave, which would be calculated in relation to the number of days or hours which they work in a week.

When a worker is on leave, they are entitled to be paid their normal rate of pay based on their normal hours of work or their contractual hours. Where, however, a worker does not have normal working hours, for example if the amount of work fluctuates, if they work irregular shift patterns, or if they are paid on the basis of piecework, then the amount payable to them during statutory leave must be calculated as an average of their actual pay during the preceding 12 weeks. This has major implications for employers whose level of work fluctuates and where employees may take leave immediately following a particularly busy period where they have worked extensive hours and received a correspondingly high level of remuneration.

Importantly, no cash substitutes for holiday not taken are allowed under the Regulations, except on termination of employment (see: *Section 10.5*). Clearly this means that employers who have adopted the practice of permitting employees to forego part of their annual holiday entitlement, and receive additional pay in lieu, must cease doing so. The aim of the Regulations is to ensure that workers receive a proper break from work from a health and safety perspective, and to ensure that the worker is paid during this break. Similarly, it is not permissible to pay workers an enhancement to their normal pay as a substitute for paid leave. There is also a rule that holidays must be taken during the year in which they are due, and not carried over to the next holiday year (*Reg 13(9)*). However, the restrictions on carry-over and pay in lieu apply only to the period of statutory leave imposed by the Regulations, and it follows that where employers grant annual leave in excess of the statutory minimum, they are free to make their own rules and arrangements regarding carry-over and pay in lieu in relation to the portion of the leave which is in excess of the statutory minimum (see: *Section 10.4*).

Public holidays are not excluded from statutory paid leave, so it may be assumed that paid public holidays can be treated as counting towards employees' statutory leave entitlement (see: *Section 10.9*).

Many employers were particularly affected by the introduction of the holiday provisions of the Regulations, especially with regard to temporary employees, casuals, freelances or those working on fixed-term contracts who, traditionally, may not have been granted paid holidays.

Workers are entitled to the minimum holiday entitlement imposed by the Regulations subject to a 13-week qualifying period of service. Thus workers engaged on a contract for less than 13 weeks do not accrue holiday entitlement under the Regulations. After the qualifying period, workers will have a right to their full leave entitlement backdated to the date their contract commenced. Part-time workers are entitled to statutory holiday under the Regulations (provided they work on a contract for more than 13 weeks) on a pro-rata basis.

The right for employees to take holidays is framed in the legislation as an entitlement rather than something which employers are compelled to force upon employees. This means that, whilst employers must not prevent employees from taking their statutory holidays, and must not penalise them for doing so, they need not force an employee to take leave if the employee chooses not to. This must, however, be the employee's choice, and not the employer's.

Special provisions exist in the Regulations relating to the timing of holidays, which give employers certain rights to regulate when workers take their statutory leave and rights may be excluded or varied by a relevant agreement (see: *Sections 9.4 and 11.4*).

Statutory holiday entitlement may be taken either in instalments or all at once.

9.2 CALCULATING HOLIDAY ENTITLEMENT FOR EMPLOYEES WHO COMMENCE EMPLOYMENT OR LEAVE PART-WAY THROUGH THE HOLIDAY YEAR

For employees who commence employment part-way through the holiday year, statutory entitlement should be calculated on a pro-rata basis, based on the number of weeks the person will be employed between their start date and the end of the company's holiday year. In other words, the entitlement of a new employee will be dependent on the amount of the leave year left when they start work. When this calculation results in a figure which includes a fraction of a day, this must be rounded up to the next whole number. The employee must be allowed to take this leave – and be paid for it – before the expiry of the holiday year. Example 9.1 illustrates this.

The same approach should be taken when an employee leaves part-way through the holiday year, but bearing in mind that fractions of days must always be rounded up.

Example 9.1

> The employer operates a holiday year which runs from 1 April to 31 March. A new employee starts work on 1 August, working 5 days per week. The calculation of the first year's statutory holiday (based on 4 weeks' statutory leave per year) will be made on the basis of 35 weeks' employment (the time period between 1 August and 31 March is 35 weeks). Thus the calculation of the new employee's holiday entitlement for the first holiday year will be made by dividing 35 by 52 and multiplying the result by 20 (the number of days' statutory holiday entitlement for the full year). The result is 13.46, which must then be rounded up to give a statutory holiday entitlement of 14 days.

9.3 CALCULATING HOLIDAY ENTITLEMENT FOR A TRANSITIONAL LEAVE YEAR

The right to statutory annual leave rose from 3 weeks to 4 on 23 November 1999. This means that, if an employee's leave year began before that date, the employer must calculate their leave entitlement taking into account a proportion of the 4th week. In other words, during a leave year which began after 23 November 1998 but before 23 November 1999, workers would have been entitled to 3 weeks' leave plus a fraction of the 4th week to take into account the portion of the holiday year that fell after 23 November 1999. Example 9.2 illustrates this.

Example 9.2

> If the holiday year runs from 1 Jan to 31 December, and assuming employees work a 5-day week, statutory holiday entitlement for 1999 will be 3 weeks plus a fraction of the 4th week. The fraction of the 4th week will be calculated by counting the number of days which fall between 23 November and 31 December (39 days), calculating that as a fraction of the total number of days in a year (365) and multiplying the resulting figure by 5 (because the employee works 5 days a week). The result is:
>
> (39 divided by 365) x 5 = 0.53 days
>
> This figure must be rounded up to the nearest day, with the result that employees' additional holiday entitlement for 1999 will be 1 day.
>
> A similar calculation based on a holiday year running from 1 April to 31 March would (based on a 5-day working week) result in the following calculation:
>
> (129 divided by 365) x 5 = 1.77
>
> This would be rounded up to give workers an additional holiday entitlement of 2 days for the holiday year running from 1 April 1999 to 31 March 2000.

9.4 TIMING OF HOLIDAYS

The *Working Time Regulations 1998* give employers some flexibility as to the timing of workers' statutory holidays.

Firstly, unless there is a workforce agreement setting out different rules, the employer is entitled to require workers to give notice in advance of taking statutory leave. The period of notice can be up to twice the number of days which the worker wishes to take as leave. Thus, for example, an employee who wished to take 2 weeks' statutory leave would be required to give their employer a maximum of 4 weeks' notice of the dates of their proposed leave.

Secondly, where a worker has given notice requesting specified days as statutory leave, it is open to the employer to refuse those days, provided the employer gives the worker counter-notice which is at least equivalent to the number of days proposed as leave. Thus, for example, where the worker has given 4 weeks' notice of a request for 2 weeks' statutory leave, the employer may refuse the dates specified by giving at least 2 weeks' counter-notice to that effect.

Thirdly, employers may, if they wish, nominate specified days on which workers must take some or all of their statutory leave. This can only be done, however, where the following conditions are met:

1   The employer must specify the days/dates in question.
2   The notice period given must equate to at least twice the number of days which the employer is specifying as statutory leave. Thus, for example, if the employer wishes to impose a 10-day shut-down at Christmas, then at least 20 days' notice of the specific dates must be provided.

The entitlement of workers to be granted 4 weeks' statutory holiday entitlement arises as soon as they have completed 13 weeks' continuous service. This means in effect that, in the absence of any contractual policy or rules to the contrary, an employee would be entitled to take their full statutory 4-week holiday entitlement once they have worked for this minimum period of 13 weeks. It is clearly advisable therefore for employers to introduce (through a workforce agreement) rules regarding the scheduling of holidays and written agreements concerning pay-back of holiday entitlement which an employee may have taken but not earned when their employment terminates (see: *Sections 10.3 and 10.5.3*).

Holiday entitlements and contracts of employment

10.1 INTRODUCTION

Prior to the introduction of legislation regulating working hours and time off rights under the *Working Time Regulations 1998*, employers were free to determine how many days' holiday (if any) to grant to their employees. There was previously no minimum or maximum entitlement in law. Under the Regulations, however, minimum periods of statutory annual leave were introduced for all workers whose contract exceeds 13 weeks. The minimum holiday entitlement is 4 weeks per annum. Further information about holiday entitlements which were imposed by the Regulations is available (see: *Chapter 9*).

A model policy on holiday entitlements and rules is available (see: *Appendix C3*).

10.2 EMPLOYEE'S RIGHT TO A WRITTEN STATEMENT OF HOLIDAY ENTITLEMENT

There is a duty on employers to provide employees with a written statement setting out the key terms and conditions of their employment (*Employment Rights Act 1996 s 1(1)*). This right accrues to all employees who continue in employment for at least 1 month; thus temporary staff engaged on a contract of less than 1 month are excluded. The written statement must be provided to employees within 2 months of commencing work (*Employment Rights Act 1996 s 1(2)*). Part-time employees have the same right in this respect as full-time staff.

The written statement must include (among other items) a statement setting out the details of the employee's holiday entitlement, including any right to public holidays, and entitlement to holiday pay (*Employment Rights Act 1996 s 1(4)(d)*). Employers may, however, wish to include fuller details in writing concerning entitlement to holidays, scheduling of holidays and other rules associated with the taking of holidays.

10.3 SCHEDULING OF HOLIDAYS

There is a requirement in the *Working Time Regulations 1998* that holidays must be taken during the year in which they are earned, and not carried over to the next holiday year (see: *Section 9.1*). However, the restrictions on carry-over apply only to the period of statutory leave imposed by the Regulations. Therefore, it follows that where employers grant contractual annual leave in excess of the statutory minimum, they are free to make their own rules and arrangements in respect of

carry-over in relation to the portion of the leave which is in excess of the statutory minimum.

Employers may wish to introduce certain contractual rules regarding the scheduling and taking of annual holidays. Common rules are:

- that employees must request annual leave dates in writing, or must follow a defined procedure;

- that the scheduling of holiday entitlement is at the discretion of management, and employees must always obtain their manager's permission before committing to any holiday arrangements;

- that no more than a fixed number of people within the same department may be away from work on holiday at the same time;

- that leave may not be taken at certain times of year;

- that some annual leave must be taken on pre-determined dates;

- that a minimum or maximum amount of leave may be taken at any one time;

- that holiday entitlement may or may not be carried forward to the following holiday year (subject to the restrictions imposed by the Regulations);

- that payment in lieu of holidays not taken may or may not be made (subject to the restrictions imposed by the Regulations);

- that holidays may or may not be taken during an employee's notice period, or that the taking of holidays during notice are at the employer's discretion.

10.3.1 Over-staying leave

Employers may sometimes wish to grant extended holiday leave to employees in certain circumstances. One common example of this is where an employee from overseas wishes to return home to visit their family, and makes a request for an extended period of leave for the visit.

It is important for employers to ensure that there is a proper, structured company policy for dealing with requests for extended leave, and clearly laid down rules and procedural steps for dealing with late returners. In this way employees will be clear about their contractual rights and fully aware of the penalties involved if they fail to return on the agreed date.

It used to be common practice for employers to enter into an agreement with employees taking extended leave in which it was agreed that failure to return on the agreed date would result in automatic termination of the employee's contract. Essentially this type of agreement was designed to prevent employees in these circumstances from claiming unfair dismissal, the argument being that the employee had effectively terminated their own employment by breaching the terms of the agreement.

This philosophy was brought to an end with the case of (*Igbo v Johnson Matthey Chemicals Ltd [1986]*) in which the Court of Appeal ruled that agreements for automatic termination of employment in these circumstances were void, because they had the effect of limiting an employee's right not to be unfairly dismissed.

See *Appendix C2* for a procedure for granting extended leave and ensuring a fair approach to dealing with the issue of late returners.

10.4 <u>PAYMENT IN LIEU OF HOLIDAYS</u>

The *Working Time Regulations 1998* state that no cash substitutes for statutory holidays not taken will be allowed, except on termination of employment (see: *Chapter 9*). Clearly this means that employers who have in the past adopted the practice of permitting employees to forego their annual holiday entitlement and receive additional pay in lieu will be compelled to cease doing so. The aim of the Regulations is to ensure that workers receive a proper break from work from a health and safety perspective, and to ensure that the worker is paid during this break. For the same reason, it is not permissible to pay workers an enhancement to their normal pay as a substitute for paid leave, or to structure pay so that part of it is deemed to be an amount paid in advance to 'cover the costs' of holidays.

This restriction on pay in lieu of holidays applies only to the period of statutory leave imposed by the Regulations. It follows, therefore, that where employers grant contractual leave in excess of the statutory minimum, they are free to make their own rules and arrangements regarding pay in lieu, in relation to the portion of leave which is in excess of the statutory minimum.

10.5 <u>PAYMENT OF ACCRUED HOLIDAYS ON TERMINATION OF EMPLOYMENT</u>

Employers should ensure that their written statements provide details of holiday entitlement which are sufficient to enable the employee's entitlement, including any entitlement to accrued holiday pay on the termination of employment, to be precisely calculated.

When an employee leaves their employment, it is normal practice for the employer to pay the person an amount of money in lieu of any holidays not taken. Although this was not, in the past, an automatic right for employees in law, the *Working Time Regulations 1998* introduced a provision that, when an employment relationship ends, an allowance must be paid to the worker in lieu of

statutory holidays not taken (*Morley v Heritage plc [1993]*). This provision only applies, however, to statutory holiday entitlement (4 weeks per annum) and not to any holiday entitlement which the employer may grant over and above the statutory minimum (see: *Chapter 9*). The payment or otherwise of holidays not taken in excess of the statutory weeks is therefore a matter for the contract of employment to determine.

It is therefore beneficial for employers to ensure that a clear statement on this matter is made either in each employee's written statement of key terms of employment, or in a separate document such as an employee handbook. This is especially important if the employer operates the practice of refusing payment for a portion of unused holidays in certain circumstances, for example where the employee leaves employment without giving proper notice under their contract, or in the event of dismissal for gross misconduct.

10.5.1 Payment of holiday pay on termination where the contract is silent

If a contract of employment is silent on the subject of holiday pay on termination of employment, an individual who is denied outstanding holiday pay would have the right to challenge the employer's decision at tribunal by claiming a breach of the holiday provisions contained in the *Working Time Regulations 1998* (for a portion of the statutory holiday entitlement).

10.5.2 Holiday pay following dismissal for gross misconduct

Where an employee is dismissed for gross misconduct, the employer could argue that, since the employee has breached a fundamental term of their employment contract entitling the employer to dismiss them, this releases the employer from any further obligations under the contract. For the avoidance of doubt, however, it is preferable for employers who wish to avoid paying outstanding holiday pay in the event of gross misconduct to include a specific clause in contracts of employment stating that holiday pay may be withheld in these circumstances. A model clause is shown below.

> If your employment is terminated on the grounds of gross misconduct, you will forego any entitlement to pay in lieu of holidays not taken.

It is unclear, however, whether it is permissible under the *Working Time Regulations 1998* to exclude an employee's right to a payment in lieu of statutory holiday entitlement earned but not taken. This is a matter which will inevitably be determined, in due course, by the courts and tribunals.

Even where a contractual clause exists entitling the employer to refuse payment of outstanding holiday pay on summary dismissal for gross misconduct, the employee could still challenge the employer's refusal on the grounds that their conduct did not constitute gross misconduct. This occurred in the case of (*Greg May (CF & C) Ltd v Dring [1990]*) when a tribunal found that an employee was entitled to the outstanding holiday pay which had been withheld from him in accordance with a clause in his contract of employment providing that accrued holiday pay would not be paid where an employee was dismissed for gross misconduct.

10.5.3 Deductions from final salary for holidays taken but not earned

If the employer wishes to operate a policy of deducting money from an employee's final salary payment for holidays which have been taken in excess of earned holiday entitlement, this may be done by means of a relevant agreement (see: *Section 11.4*) covering this specific point. A properly worded clause in each individual's contract of employment would be sufficient to authorise this. This position could arise, for example, where an employee took 2 or more weeks' holiday early in the year, and then left employment during the summer. A model clause is shown below.

> If you resign from your employment, or are dismissed for any reason whatsoever, whether with or without notice, the employer reserves the right to deduct from your final salary payment an amount of money equivalent to any paid statutory or contractual holiday leave which you have taken in excess of your earned entitlement for the current holiday year.

It is unlawful to deduct money from an employee's wages without specific written authorisation obtained from the employee in advance (*Employment Rights Act 1996 s 13*).

The *Working Time Regulations 1998* specify that, where there is a relevant agreement to authorise it, the employer may claim compensation from an employee who is leaving for holiday entitlement taken in excess of the statutory entitlement.

10.6 <u>HOLIDAYS AND SICKNESS ABSENCE</u>

One aspect of company policy which can cause confusion is whether employees who fall sick while on holiday should be transferred to sick leave and paid

company sick pay or statutory sick pay (SSP). The implications of this for the employee would be that they would be eligible to take the holiday they have lost through sickness at a later date.

This is a matter for the employer to determine and communicate to employees as a contractual issue. Some employers operate a discretionary policy whereby illness of more than a defined period (for example, 1 week) will render the employee eligible to transfer to sick leave, provided the illness is fully certificated by a qualified medical practitioner. Where an employer operates such a policy, it is recommended that it should be conditional on three factors:

- that there must be a defined minimum number of days certified sickness for the employee to qualify;

- that the employee notifies the company at the earliest opportunity that they are ill;

- that the employee provides a doctor's certificate covering the whole period of sickness.

See *Appendix C3* for a model policy which covers this point.

10.7 <u>HOLIDAYS AND MATERNITY LEAVE</u>

All employees, whether full- or part-time, are entitled to take a period of up to 18 weeks' ordinary maternity leave and resume work (*Employment Rights Act 1996 s 73*). There is no requirement for a woman to have a minimum period of qualifying service to qualify for ordinary maternity leave.

During ordinary maternity leave, the woman's contract of employment continues in force and there is no question of the contract being suspended. It follows, therefore, that the employer is obliged to continue to provide the employee with all her normal benefits under the contract, except remuneration (*Employment Rights Act 1996 s 71*). Thus holiday entitlement must be allowed to continue to accrue throughout an employee's period of ordinary maternity leave.

Because a woman's contract of employment subsists during ordinary maternity leave, any failure to maintain contractual benefits would constitute a breach of contract. Failure to continue benefits would also constitute direct sex discrimination.

Entitlement to additional maternity leave accrues to employees who have at least 1 year's continuous service calculated as at 11 weeks before their baby is due. Entitlement is to take maternity leave of up to 40 weeks in total, consisting of up to 11 weeks before the date the baby is due, and up to 29 weeks after the confinement.

During additional maternity leave, the employee's contract of employment is deemed to continue in force. However, further holiday accrual need not be granted in respect of the period beyond the initial 18 weeks of ordinary maternity leave.

Irrespective of a woman's statutory entitlements, some employers' contracts of employment may confer the right to the continuation of contractual benefits during additional maternity leave.

10.8 RELIGIOUS HOLIDAYS

Where employees of a minority racial or ethnic group wish to take part of their annual holiday entitlement at certain times of year in order to celebrate a particular religious festival, the employer should give fair and open consideration to such a request, and not dismiss it out of hand. This is because a refusal which cannot be justified on objective job-based grounds could give rise to claims of indirect race discrimination (*J H Walker Ltd v Hussain & ors [1995]*).

Although discrimination on the grounds of religion is not unlawful in England, Wales and Scotland, in certain circumstances unfavourable treatment of an employee on the grounds of religion may constitute indirect race discrimination against a particular racial group (*Race Relations Act 1976 s 1(1)(b)*). This is because, in certain circumstances, people who are members of a particular religious group may be able to show that their group has a sufficient number of relevant characteristics for it to constitute a group with separate ethnic origins (*Race Relations Act 1976 s 3(1)*). An example could be a group of Muslims, who, although not regarded as a racial group per se in the context of the Race Relations Act 1976, could be regarded as a separate group on the grounds of nationality if the majority of the particular group within the particular employment originated from Pakistan (for example).

10.9 PUBLIC HOLIDAYS

There is no general right in law for employees to be granted public holidays, nor to be paid at an enhanced rate of pay if a public holiday is worked. Special provisions are in place for banks and other financial institutions.

The public holidays commonly recognised by banks and other financial institutions are those which are laid down in the *Banking and Financial Dealings Act 1971*. This Act, however, only applies directly to banks and certain other financial institutions, and holds that these institutions are permitted to close on

certain days. The Act does not confer any rights on the employees of those institutions to time off on the nominated public holidays, whether paid or unpaid.

Holiday entitlement beyond the statutory minimum (4 weeks per annum) imposed by the *Working Time Regulations 1998* is part of an employee's contract of employment, thus entitlement to a day off (paid or unpaid) on a bank holiday depends on the specific terms of the employee's contract. The same principle applies to an employee's entitlement to extra payment, or a day's holiday in lieu, where a bank holiday is worked.

Employers are therefore free to decide which public holidays, if any, are recognised, whether or not the business should close, and whether or not employees should be granted time off with pay on the nominated days. Paid public holidays, when granted, can be used to count towards workers' entitlement to statutory paid annual leave under the Regulations.

Whatever the employer's policy is, the written statement of key terms of employment should provide full details of employees' holiday entitlements (*Employment Rights Act 1996 s 1(4)(d)*).

Employers may wish to bear in mind that, traditionally, public holidays differ in the various constituent countries within the UK (i.e. England, Scotland, Northern Ireland and Wales), and in Scotland some public holidays vary from region to region.

See *Appendix C3* for a model policy covering holiday entitlements, including public holidays.

Part IV

Administration and Contracting out

Employer–employee agreements

11.1 INTRODUCTION

There are a number of provisions of the *Working Time Regulations 1998* which can be modified by employers by setting up an agreement. The practical effect of this is that employers may modify the way in which the Regulations apply to them in certain defined areas.

There are three types of possible agreement:

- a collective agreement (see: *Section 11.2*);
- a workforce agreement (see: *Section 11.3*);
- a relevant agreement (see: *Section 11.4*).

11.2 COLLECTIVE AGREEMENTS

A collective agreement has the usual meaning, i.e. an agreement made with an independent trade union by an employer or employers' association.

11.3 WORKFORCE AGREEMENTS

Whether there is a recognised trade union or not, an employer may reach a workforce agreement with appropriate elected representatives. Essentially the provision to enter into a workforce agreement provides employers who do not recognise a trade union with a non-union route to collective negotiation.

A workforce agreement must be signed (before it comes into effect):

- by all the representatives of the workforce or of the particular group; or
- if the employer employs 20 or fewer workers, either by all the representatives or by the majority of workers.

A workforce agreement must:

- be in writing;
- have effect for a period of time which is specified and which does not exceed 5 years;
- apply to either the whole workforce or a defined group within the workforce.

All employees covered by a workforce agreement have the right to receive a copy of the workforce agreement and appropriate guidance notes to enable them to understand it fully.

It is open to the employer to decide how many representatives are to be elected for this purpose. Employers may wish to make use of existing elected representatives (elected for another purpose such as health and safety consultation) for the purpose of setting up a workforce agreement. However, before doing so, the employer must be sure that their election meets the requirements in the Regulations (*Working Time Regulations 1998 Sch para 3*). Representatives have automatic protection under the Regulations against dismissal or any detriment imposed as a consequence of their standing for, or acting as, a representative.

11.4 RELEVANT AGREEMENTS

This type of agreement is a catch-all category, and the term 'relevant agreement' includes collective agreements, workforce agreements and individual agreements with workers. This is because the definition of 'relevant agreement' in the *Working Time Regulations 1998* is:

> "a workforce agreement which applies to [the worker], any provision of a collective agreement which forms part of a contract between him and his employer, or any other agreement in writing which is legally enforceable as between the worker and his employer."

The key features are that the agreement must be in writing and must genuinely be an agreement, as opposed to a written document which is simply issued by the employer to the workers. A new employee's (written) contract of employment would be valid as a relevant agreement in this context for that individual.

11.5 ISSUES OVER WHICH AGREEMENTS CAN BE REACHED

Issues over which relevant agreements may have influence include:

1 Modification or exclusion of the provisions in the *Working Time Regulations 1998* covering length of rest periods and length of night work (*Reg 21*, see: *Chapters 4 and 6*). The key limitation on this provision is that, where workers are not given the daily or weekly rest breaks laid down in the Regulations, they must be granted equivalent periods of compensatory rest.

2 The start dates for the reference periods used to calculate average working hours (see: *Chapter 3*). If no agreement is in place a rolling reference period will apply.

3 For certain categories of worker, the length of the reference period for calculating average working hours, which can be extended to 52 weeks.

4 The length of notice which a worker must provide to the employer to cancel an agreement under which the individual volunteered to work longer than 48 hours per week (see: *Section 3.3*). The default period of notice (if no relevant agreement is in place) is 7 days.

5 The length of the rest break during the day for workers whose working day exceeds 6 hours (see: *Section 4.2*). The default length is 20 minutes.

6 The day of the week on which a week starts for the purpose of calculating weekly rest periods (see: *Section 4.4*). The default is Sunday at midnight.

7 The definition of night time, i.e. the start and end of the period which is to be regarded as night time (see: *Section 6.2*). Where no agreement is in place which deals with this issue, the default period is from 11.00 p.m. to 6.00 a.m.

8 The type of night work which is to be regarded as involving special hazards or heavy physical or mental strain (see: *Section 6.5*).

9 Rules under which an employer can compel a worker to take statutory leave on dates specified by the employer.

10 Notice periods required for the purpose of agreeing the dates on which workers should take their statutory annual leave (see: *Section 9.4*).

11 The start and end of the holiday year for the purpose of statutory annual leave. Without an agreement covering this issue, the holiday year will commence either on 1 October (the date the Regulations came into effect), or on each individual's start date.

12 The right of the employer to claw back statutory holiday entitlement taken by an employee who leaves before having earned this entitlement (see: *Section 10.5.3*).

It is clearly in the interests of employers to set up relevant agreements to cover some or all of these issues. Complete disarray could ensue if, for example, there is no relevant agreement establishing when the holiday year starts – in which case the employer would have to calculate each new worker's holiday entitlement in accordance with their individual start date. Similar administrative confusion could occur if there was no relevant agreement covering the start and end dates of the reference periods used to calculate average working hours.

Record keeping and enforcement

12.1 <u>RECORD KEEPING</u>

As part of the enforcement of the *Working Time Regulations 1998*, records of relevant agreements and working hours must be made available for inspection by the Health and Safety Executive (HSE) who may, for reasons connected with the health or safety of the worker, prohibit or restrict the possibility of working hours exceeding 48 per week (see: *Section 12.2.1*). Employers are compelled to co-operate with such officials.

Records must include:

1 Details of any relevant agreements entered into between the employer and the workforce for the purposes of modifying the application of the Regulations.

2 Details of each worker who has signed an individual written agreement to work in excess of an average of 48 hours per week.

3 The terms on which the worker agreed that the 48-hour limit would not apply.

4 Information about employees' working hours which is sufficient to show that the Regulations have been complied with. The requirement for employers to maintain detailed records of the hours of every opted-out worker was abolished in December 1999 (*Working Time Regulations 1999 Reg 3*).

5 For night workers, full records of night-time hours going back at least 2 years and maintained in sufficient detail to enable the authorities to determine whether the limit on length of night work is being complied with in relation to each worker.

12.1.1 Monitoring employees' working hours

It is up to each employer to determine the form and style of their records, and the design of their system of monitoring. Where, for example, employees are paid by the hour, then existing pay records will probably be sufficient to demonstrate each worker's actual working hours.

Where workers never work more than, for example, 40 hours per week, then, provided each worker's contract specifies a 40-hour week, it may be sufficient to use a management system to ensure that actual working hours are in accordance with the contract. However, the management system would have to be organised so that it would highlight any instance where a worker worked in excess of their contractual working hours, so some monitoring would be inevitable.

12.2 <u>ENFORCEMENT</u>

The *Working Time Regulations 1998* are subject to a variety of enforcement measures. These can be summarised as follows:

- workers' rights to complain to an employment tribunal if their rights have been breached (see: *Section 12.2.1*);
- criminal sanctions (see: *Section 12.2.2*);
- enforcement by the Health and Safety Executive (see: *Section 12.2.3*);
- claims by workers for breach of contract (see: *Section 12.2.4*).

12.2.1 Employee's right to complain to an employment tribunal

Individual employees who believe their entitlements have been breached can take a complaint to an employment tribunal. There is no minimum length of service required for an employee to take this course of action, and a dismissal which is found to have been on the grounds of breach of the *Working Time Regulations 1998* will be automatically unfair. The types of complaint which an individual is permitted to take to tribunal include:

- refusal of the employer to grant minimum daily or weekly rest periods;
- refusal of the employer to grant statutory annual leave, or refusal to pay for such leave;
- being subjected to any detriment for refusing to agree to work more than an average of 48 hours per week, insisting on the right to take rest breaks, or refusing to sign a workforce agreement;
- dismissal for refusing to agree to work more than an average of 48 hours per week, insisting on the right to take rest breaks or refusing to sign a workforce agreement;
- being dismissed or subjected to a detriment for being a candidate in an election for workplace representatives, or for carrying out the activities of an elected representative;
- dismissal for alleging in good faith that the employer contravened a right under the Regulations.

12.2.2 Criminal offences

In addition to the rights of individuals to enforce their entitlements under the *Working Time Regulations 1998*, the Regulations contain provisions to make it a criminal offence for an employer to breach the working time limits. Working time

is regarded as a health and safety issue, and the Regulations are thus capable of being enforced in the same way as other health and safety regulations. Thus an employer who breaches the Regulations may be convicted of an offence punishable by a fine or even imprisonment, as is normal for health and safety offences.

12.2.3 Inspection of employers' records by the Health and Safety Executive

The HSE is entitled to carry out inspections of employers' records and, where appropriate, issue improvement or prohibition notices to compel employers to comply with the *Working Time Regulations 1998*.

12.2.4 Breach of contract

There has been an interesting development with regard to employees' rights to restrict their working hours to a maximum average of 48 hours per week. A group of pit deputies who worked in coal mines in Yorkshire had had pressure exerted on them to agree to volunteer to opt out of the 48-hour limit. Although none of the employees in question had signed an opt-out agreement, the hours they had in practice worked were greatly in excess of 48 on average.

In the High Court in England the employees argued that their employer had a contractual duty under the *Working Time Regulations 1998* not to require or expect them to work more than an average of 48 hours per week in any reference period. The Court upheld their case, taking the view that the Regulations created a free-standing contractual right for employees to restrict their working hours to no more than an average of 48 per week, and that any infringement of that right would constitute a breach of contract (*Barber & ors v RJB Mining (UK) Ltd, High Court 03.03.99*).

The outcome was that the pit deputies, who had worked more than an average of 48 hours per week during the previous 17 weeks, obtained a declaration to the effect that they could not be required by their employer to work any more hours at all until sufficient time had elapsed to bring their weekly average hours within the specified limit.

Proposed future working time provisions from Europe

13.1 <u>INTRODUCTION</u>

Measures to extend the terms of working hours legislation to those who are excluded from the scope of the Working Time Directive have been agreed in Europe. The view was held that existing legislation does not go far enough in securing protection for employees from a health and safety perspective. The implementation period for measures affecting transport workers, sea fishermen and offshore workers will be 4 years, while for junior doctors a 9-year implementation period is proposed.

Thus the categories of worker who are currently excluded from the provisions of the Working Time Directive (see: *Section 2.4.1*), in particular junior doctors, transport workers, sea fishing workers and offshore workers, will be covered by future legislation.

13.2 <u>DETAILS OF THE PROPOSALS</u>

The new proposals include the following:

1 All non-mobile workers in the transport sector are to be confirmed as falling within the scope of the existing Working Time Directive (whether or not such workers are covered by the *Working Time Regulations 1998* has been disputed since the Regulations were introduced).

2 Mobile workers in the road, air and inland waterway transport sector will have a statutory right to limit working hours over a period of a year, the right to adequate rest periods and the right to 4 weeks' paid annual leave.

3 Workers in the road haulage industry will be covered by a new Directive, which is likely to provide for a maximum working week of 48 hours averaged over a reference period of 4 months (extendable in certain circumstances). This Directive will also impose an absolute maximum working week of 60 hours, and give workers entitlement to weekly and daily rest periods.

4 There is a proposal for a new Directive to cover people who work at sea. The Directive will reflect the provisions of the ILO Convention No 180 on seafarers' hours of work. This provides for either a maximum number of working hours (14 hours in any 24-hour period and 72 hours in any 7-day period) or for minimum rest periods (10 hours in any 24-hour period and 77 hours in any 7-day period).

5 The current Working Time Directive is to be amended to cover junior doctors in training, mobile railway workers and offshore workers in the oil and gas exploration industry. The current maximum average weekly limit of 48 hours per week will eventually apply to junior doctors, although this is to be phased in over a 4-year transitional period.

Frequently asked questions

1 Does the legislation on working time mean that employees cannot be allowed to work longer than 48 hours per week?

It is unlawful under the *Working Time Regulations 1998* to impose a contractual requirement on an employee to work more than 48 hours per week on average, or to compel someone to work longer than 48 hours a week on average against their will (see: *Chapter 3*). Employees may, however, be permitted to volunteer to work more than 48 hours per week on average (see: *Section 3.3*).

2 What are the compulsory rest periods imposed by the Working Time Regulations?

The rest periods imposed by the Regulations are a compulsory daily rest period of at least 11 consecutive hours every 24 hours, a weekly rest period of at least 24 hours (which may be averaged over 2 weeks), and a 20 minute rest break during the working day where it exceeds 6 hours (see: *Chapter 4*).

3 Which workers are exempted from the provisions on working hours?

Certain categories of worker are totally exempted from the scope of the provisions (*Reg 18*, see: *Section 2.4.1*). These are junior doctors, certain forces and police personnel, transport workers, sea fishing workers, and other people who are engaged in work at sea. Additionally, workers with autonomous decision-taking powers, e.g. managing executives, are exempted from the 48-hour restriction and the provisions on rest breaks and night working (*Reg 21*, see: *Section 2.4.2*).

4 When is a worker to be regarded as a 'night worker' in relation to the provisions in the Working Time Regulations which restrict night-time hours?

An employee is classed as a night worker if they work 3 or more hours during night time (as a normal course) (*Reg 2*, see: *Section 6.3*). 'Normal course' is defined such that someone who works at least 3 hours during night time on the majority of their working days will be classed as a night worker, even if they divide their time between day and night shift working. A worker may also be regarded as a night worker if they work 'a certain proportion of their annual working time' during night time.

5 How precisely must an employer define an employee's working hours in the contract of employment?

The written statement of key terms and conditions of employment should include the employee's normal hours of work (if there are specified normal working hours), overtime requirements and any flexibility which is required (*Employment Rights Act 1996 s 1(4)(c)*, see: *Section 7.2*).

It is not necessary for the employer to state specific hours of work in the written statement although employers may do this if they wish. If the employer wishes an employee to work variable hours, then the written statement can specify this. The written statement may even say that the employee is required to work any reasonable number of hours according to the needs of the job.

6 Why might a requirement for extensive overtime working discriminate against women?

It has been generally accepted by the courts that women are less able to comply with a requirement to work long hours than men (because in general more family responsibilities fall to women than to men). Thus a requirement for extensive overtime could place a female employee at a disadvantage if she was unable to comply with the hours required of her owing to domestic or child-minding responsibilities. Unless the employer can justify the requirement on objective, job-based grounds, this could amount to indirect sex discrimination in law (*Sex Discrimination Act 1975 s 1(1)(b)*, see: *Section 7.4*).

7 In what circumstances can an employer alter employees' working hours?

Employers may only alter employees' working hours if there is a flexibility clause in the contract of employment specifically entitling them to do so, or if the employee has expressly agreed to the change. The employer may in certain circumstances be able to achieve employee agreement by going though a process of consultation, provided that there are sound business reasons for the proposed changes (see: *Chapter 8*). A procedure to achieve this is given in *Appendix C1*.

8 What provisions do the Working Time Regulations make with regard to employees' holiday entitlements?

Workers are entitled to a minimum of 4 weeks' paid annual leave. No cash substitutes are allowed in lieu of holidays not taken, except on termination of employment, and employees must be granted holidays during the holiday year in which they are earned (see: *Chapter 9*).

9 What is the position in law with regard to payment of accrued holiday entitlement on termination of employment?

Any statutory holiday entitlement earned under the Working Time Regulations but not taken must be paid for on termination of employment. Beyond that, the payment or

otherwise of holidays not taken is a matter for the contract of employment to determine (see: *Section 10.5*).

10 How many public holidays per year are employees entitled to receive?

There is no general right in law for employees to be granted time off on public holidays, nor to be paid at an enhanced rate of pay if a public holiday is worked (see: *Section 10.9*). Employers are therefore free to decide which public holidays, if any, are recognised, whether or not the business should close, and whether or not employees should be granted time off with pay on the nominated days.

Problem solvers

Problem 1

Employees who want to carry on working more than 48 hours per week

Our company has several employees who consistently work more than 48 hours per week, and thus earn substantial overtime payments. This practice suits the company, and the employees value the additional income. Now that the *Working Time Regulations 1998* have been introduced into UK law, are we compelled to restrict the employees' hours of work to 48 hours per week?

Cure

The provisions of the Regulations allow for employees to volunteer to work longer than 48 hours per week (see: *Section 3.3*). Thus employees who are keen to earn overtime, and who wish to work longer than 48 hours per week, may be permitted to do so, provided they sign individual written agreements and a record of them is maintained by the employer.

It is important to remember, however, that workers must not be required or pressurised by their employer to work more than 48 hours per week, and must not be subjected to any detriment for refusing to agree to work more than 48 hours per week, or for withdrawing from their opt-out agreement.

Prevention

It would be in your interests to carry out an audit of all employees' actual working time in order to identify who regularly works in excess of 48 hours per week on average. Each individual who does so must have signed an agreement indicating their willingness to do so. A full audit will provide you with a solid basis for determining what action is required to ensure compliance with the Regulations.

Work in excess of 48 hours per week is only permissible if a proper record is kept of the workers who have signed an opt-out agreement, and the terms on which it has been agreed that the 48-hour limit will not apply. (see: *Chapter 12*). The records must be available for inspection by the Health and Safety Executive.

Problem 2

Night shift working

We operate a shift system which involves a night shift commencing at 8.00 p.m. and finishing at 6.00 a.m. Employees on night shift usually work 4 nights per week, totalling 40 hours. We are uncertain how the provisions of the Working Time

Regulations affect us. Our employees work less than 48 hours per week on average, but we understand there are also restrictions on night working. How will these affect our shift pattern?

Cure

The Working Time Directive, as a health and safety measure, imposed restrictions on night working (see: *Chapter 6*). There is a general provision in the Regulations for a maximum night shift of 8 hours, which may be averaged over a reference period of 17 weeks (longer in certain circumstances). Certain categories of worker may be exempted from the night shift restrictions, for example where the work cannot be interrupted on technical grounds (see: *Section 6.7*). As long as your employees' contracts provide for them to work only 4 nights per week at 10 hours per night, the averaging mechanism ensures that you remain within the scope of the law. This is because the night-working provisions relate to normal or contractual night hours (unlike the provisions governing the 48-hour week, which relate to actual hours worked).

Prevention

Employers who operate shift systems are advised to review those systems as an immediate priority, and to review whether any changes are required as a result of the Regulations. Where change is necessary, time should be allowed for proper consultation and discussion of the most acceptable alternatives.

Problem 3

Statutory holiday entitlements for workers on a fixed-term contract

We frequently employ project staff on fixed-term contracts, usually for 2 or 3 years. It has not been our practice to offer paid holidays to these staff as their presence at work is fairly critical at certain times during the projects. We do, however, pay them an enhanced rate of pay to compensate them for this. Can we continue this practice of buying out holiday entitlement following the introduction of the Working Time Regulations?

Cure

Essentially, no. The Regulations prescribe 4 weeks' paid holiday entitlement with no cash substitutes being allowed, except during the year of termination of employment (see: *Chapter 9*). This means that holidays must be taken during the holiday year in which they are earned, and not allowed to accrue or be bought out. The aim of the Regulations is to ensure that workers receive a proper break from work from a health and safety perspective.

Prevention

Employers who have adopted the practice of permitting employees to forego their annual holiday entitlement, and receive additional pay in lieu, should cease doing so as a result of the introduction of the Regulations. It would be advisable to draft and communicate a policy to that effect as soon as possible so that management can plan ahead and properly manage employees' holiday breaks in the future.

Problem 4

Altering working hours

We are a small business which is expanding, and we wish to open our premises to customers during evenings up to 8.00 p.m. To achieve this successfully, we will require some of our employees to change their working hours to cover the evening shift. The normal working day according to existing contracts of employment is from 9.00 a.m. to 5.00 p.m. Can we alter the employees' working hours in these circumstances, so that they start work later, and finish at 8.00 p.m.?

Cure

In the absence of a flexibility clause with regard to working hours, you cannot simply impose a change of hours on your employees. To do so against their will would be a breach of contract.

You should consult your employees in order to seek their agreement to a change in working hours. If, following consultations, employees still refuse to agree to the proposed changes, then you could terminate the existing contracts of employment (with notice) and offer re-engagement on the new terms with the new contracts running consecutively with the old (see: *Chapter 8*). A procedure detailing how to do this is given in *Appendix C1*.

Prevention

You can prevent this problem arising in the future by ensuring that all new employees have a suitably worded flexibility clause in their contracts of employment (see: *Section 8.4*).

It is important to note that the flexibility clause must cover the specific type of alteration of the working hours which the employer wishes to introduce. Usually there are two key issues:

- the number of working hours per week, and

- the timing of working, e.g. shift working and which days of the week are worked.

You should carefully review what type of flexibility will be required from employees and ensure that a clearly drafted clause covering the type of flexibility you need is written into employees' contracts of employment at the outset of employment.

Problem 5

Outstanding holiday pay on termination of employment in the case of gross misconduct by an employee

We have recently dismissed an employee for gross misconduct, without notice or pay in lieu. She had 2 weeks' outstanding holiday entitlement due to her for this year. She is arguing that she is entitled to receive pay in lieu of these holidays, and we have refused to pay. Who is right?

Cure

The Regulations specify that workers are entitled, on termination of employment, to receive an allowance in lieu of statutory holidays earned but not taken. In these circumstances, the payment or otherwise of holidays (in excess of statutory holidays) not taken on termination of employment is a matter for the contract of employment to determine. If there is no clause in the contract specifying that outstanding holiday will be paid to employees when they leave, you would have good grounds for refusing to pay. But if the contract does say that you will pay for untaken holiday, a claim to an employment tribunal for the outstanding holiday pay would probably succeed.

Prevention

It is beneficial for employers to ensure that a clear statement on holiday pay on termination of employment is made either in each employee's written statement of key terms of employment, or in a relevant agreement (see: *Section 10.5*). This is especially important if you wish to refuse payment for unused holidays in circumstances of dismissal for gross misconduct, or in other instances, for example where the employee leaves employment without giving proper notice under their contract. A model policy covering holiday entitlements and rules is given in *Appendix C3*.

Appendix C

Policies and procedures

C1 Procedure for altering employees' working hours

Where no flexibility clause exists within a contract of employment entitling the employer to alter working hours or shift patterns, and where employees have not agreed to the proposed changes, the employer should proceed as follows to introduce the desired changes:

1 Consider whether the proposal to make changes to working hours is in fact one for which there are sound business reasons, and not just administrative convenience.

2 Consult trade union representatives or employee representatives about the proposed changes at an early stage.

3 Make an individual offer (in writing) to every employee affected to vary the contract of employment, and fully explain the proposals and their reasons. It should be made clear at this stage that what is being put forward is a proposal and not a non-negotiable statement of intent.

4 If employees refuse to accept the new terms, hold discussions and listen to their reasons for rejecting the proposals. Some of the problems raised may be of such a nature that solutions can be found. For example, an employee may object to working a later shift on the grounds that there is no public transport enabling them to get home. The employer may be able to overcome this problem by offering to provide the employee with transport home (for example, a taxi). Thus the employer should act reasonably and take reasonable steps to overcome any objections raised by the employees in connection with the proposed changes. Employees should, however, be made aware at this stage (as well as later on – see below) that a continued refusal to agree to the proposed changes could lead to their dismissal.

5 Consultation may be with individual employees, with employee representatives, or with trade union representatives, so long as all affected employees are given the opportunity to learn of the employer's proposals and put forward their views. The consultation period should be on the same time-terms as redundancy consultation, i.e. a minimum of 30 days where 20 or more people are affected and a minimum of 90 days where 100 people or more are affected. Where fewer than 20 people are involved, as much consultation as is reasonably practicable should be undertaken.

6 Follow up the consultations in writing, recording the position, noting any particular objections and specifying any other options which might be explored. Employees should be sent individual letters at all stages of the consultation process.

7 Send employees who have still refused to agree to the changes a letter warning them that the consequence of their continued refusal to co-operate could be termination of their existing contract of employment, and an offer of re-engagement on the revised hours/new shift pattern. Employees should be given one final opportunity to reconsider their position. It is important to make it clear that this notice will be notice of termination of the contract, and not notice of a variation to the terms of the existing contract.

8 Ultimately, where employees still refuse to agree to the proposed change, write to them terminating their contracts of employment with proper notice, and at the same time offer re-engagement on the revised terms. Inform employees that if they accept the new contract, their employment will be continuous without loss of any statutory or contractual rights.

9 At all times behave reasonably towards employees.

10 Those employees who decline the new offer will be effectively dismissed, so they should not be allowed back into work or paid after the expiry date unless they sign up. Dismissed employees would have the right, subject to a minimum of 1 year's service, to take a claim for unfair dismissal to an employment tribunal. Provided there were sound business reasons for the change to start with, an employee's refusal to accept a reasonable offer of changed terms will generally amount to reasonable grounds for dismissal (under the heading of 'some other substantial reason'). The employer's defence to any claims of unfair dismissal will be especially strengthened if a substantial number of affected employees have been prepared to go along with the changes. Furthermore, provided the employer has gone through an adequate process of consultation and communication (as suggested above), and has acted fairly and reasonably throughout, then the consequent dismissals are likely to be fair.

C2 Procedure for granting extended leave and dealing with employees who return from leave late

Managers who are responsible for granting and controlling extended leave should follow the guidelines set out below:

1 Ensure that any policy on extended leave is clearly drafted and communicated to all employees.

2 If the policy is discretionary, ensure it is used fairly and that employees are treated consistently.

3 Ensure employees are fully advised of any conditions attached to the granting of extended leave, and the likely consequences of a failure to return on time.

4 Obtain an employee's signature at the commencement of extended leave to indicate their acceptance of the terms of granting the leave, and the rules.

5 If an employee fails to return from leave on the agreed date, investigate thoroughly to try to establish what happened.

6 If the employee is away from home and cannot be contacted, take all possible steps to get word to them and wait a reasonable period of time before deciding to dismiss. Avoid acting hastily.

7 Take into account any medical certificates sent in or other available medical evidence. Treat any foreign medical certificates as equivalent to those from UK doctors, otherwise there could be an inference of racial discrimination. One option would be to take steps to verify they are genuine by contacting the doctor or institution.

8 Take all reasonable steps to attempt to contact the employee before reaching any decision.

9 Where the employee can be contacted, ensure they are given a fair hearing in order to establish the reason for the late return.

10 Be aware that a termination of employment as result of late return from leave is a dismissal in law. If the employee takes a case of unfair dismissal to employment tribunal, the employer will have to show not only that there was a fair reason for the dismissal, but also that a fair procedure was followed under all the circumstances of the particular case.

C3 Policy on annual holidays

This policy, which forms part of employees' terms and conditions of employment, is intended to provide employees with a clear understanding of their entitlements to annual holidays and public holidays, and to explain their obligations under the policy.

Entitlement to annual holiday

The company's holiday year runs from 1 January to 31 December each year. All full-time employees of the company are entitled to 4 weeks' (20 working days') paid holiday per annum, plus public holidays (see below). You will be paid at your normal salary (average wage) during annual holidays, i.e. your rate of pay exclusive of overtime (commission/bonus). Part-time employees have the same entitlement to holidays as full-time staff, based pro rata on the number of days or part days worked per week.

Workers who are not employees of the company will also be entitled to 4 weeks' paid holiday entitlement per annum, paid at their normal rate of pay.

The following sections of this policy, except for the last one, also apply to non-employed workers. However, the final section of this policy, in relation to public holidays, does not apply to those who are not direct employees of the company, and no additional time off or pay in lieu of public holidays worked will be granted over and above the 4 weeks' paid holiday entitlement.

(Alternative clause) The following sections of this policy also apply to non-employed workers.

Holiday entitlement during holiday year of joining the company

On joining the company, entitlement to paid holiday will be pro rated to 1.66 days per month left in the holiday year. Where this results in a part-day entitlement, the resulting figure will be rounded up to the nearest whole number in order to calculate the total entitlement for that year. However, only complete months will be counted for holiday entitlement purposes.

Holiday entitlement on termination of employment

Similarly, the employee's entitlement during the holiday year in which employment terminates will be calculated on the basis of 1.66 days per month worked (only complete months will be counted). Any outstanding holiday entitlement will normally be paid to you along with your final salary payment. Such payment is taxable and subject to national insurance deductions. Where you wish to take outstanding holiday during the notice period, this will be granted wherever possible. However, such a request cannot be guaranteed as the granting of holidays in these circumstances depends on operational requirements, the need for outstanding work to be completed, and the need for a handover to a successor.

There are two exceptions to the rule regarding holiday pay on termination. In either of the following circumstances you will forego any entitlement to pay in lieu of holidays not taken:

- if your employment is terminated by the company on the grounds of gross misconduct, or

- if you leave the company without giving proper notice under your contract of employment.

If, at the time your employment terminates, you have taken more holidays than you have earned, then the company reserves the right to deduct the equivalent amount of money (at a rate equivalent to your normal basic salary) from your final salary payment.

Authorisation of holidays

Holidays may be taken at any time of year, subject to your manager's agreement. You are required to obtain your line manager's written approval before taking any holidays, and, where your proposed holiday is for a period of 1 week or more, to give at least 4 weeks' notice before the beginning of your holiday. For periods of leave of less than 1 week, you are required to give notice of at least twice the amount of holiday you propose to take, e.g. if you are applying for 1 day's leave, you must give at least 2 days' notice. Authorisation should be sought by completing the 'holiday request form' available from your manager or personnel department. In extreme emergencies, holidays may be granted where 4 weeks' notice has not been given.

Your line manager will return the holiday request form to you within 3 days marked 'approved' or 'not approved'. If your request for specific dates has not been approved, the reason for the refusal will be given. You should on no account commit yourself to any holiday plans before receiving approval for your holiday dates.

The company cannot guarantee to grant your chosen holiday dates. Generally it will not be possible to allow more than two employees from the same department to be on holiday at the same time. The system therefore operates on a first-come, first-served basis, and it follows that the sooner you register your holiday request form, the more likely it is that you will be granted the dates you seek. [Alternatively, employers may wish to give priority to parents of school-age children for holiday dates during school holidays, although, it should be noted that this could cause unrest and dissatisfaction amongst childless employees.]

There is no minimum, and no maximum, number of days' holiday which may be taken at one time.

Illness during holidays

If you are ill while on holiday for a period of more than 7 (calendar) days, the company may elect, at its discretion, to regard your absence as sickness leave. This will be the case only where the company is satisfied your sickness is genuine and where:

- you notify the company at the earliest opportunity that you are ill;

- you provide a doctor's certificate covering the whole period of sickness.

Where your absence is accepted as sickness absence, you will receive [company sick pay/SSP] according to the company's policy governing sick pay. You will then be permitted to take the holiday you have lost at a later date, subject to agreement with your line manager on the dates the holiday is to be taken.

Periods of sickness during holidays lasting less than 7 days and any periods of uncertificated absence will not entitle you to claim sickness absence, and will continue to be regarded as annual holiday.

Carrying over of holidays

The company does not permit employees to carry over holidays from one year to the next as this is prohibited by the *Working Time Regulations 1998*. All holidays must be taken during the year in which they are earned. Payment in lieu of holidays not taken may be made only upon termination of employment.

Line managers are expected to ensure that all employees in their department plan and take their full holiday entitlement, and that holiday absences are spread reasonably evenly throughout the year in order to avoid undue disruption to the company's business.

Public holidays

The company recognises eight public holidays a year, the dates of which vary from year to year. Each year, a notice will be placed on the notice-board at the beginning of the year stating the dates on which the public holidays fall for that year.

You will normally be granted a day's paid holiday on each public holiday nominated by the company. This is in addition to your annual holiday entitlement.

If you are asked to work on a nominated public holiday, it is a condition of your employment that you agree to do so. In this case you will be offered either:

- another [day off/2 days off] in lieu, the date of which is to be agreed with your line manager, or

- an extra day's pay at [single time/double time], based on your normal rate of pay.

You may choose whichever of the two options you prefer.

Where a public holiday falls within your approved annual leave, an additional day's holiday will be added to your annual holiday entitlement.

To qualify for payment for a public holiday, you must satisfy one of the following criteria:

- you must work up until normal finishing time on the last working day before the public holiday, and must return to work at the normal starting time on the first working day after the holiday, or
- you must be on approved annual leave on the working day before and the working day after the public holiday, or
- you must have provided a doctor's certificate confirming you are unable to attend work on the working day before, and the working day after, the public holiday.

Unauthorised absence on the working day immediately before, or immediately after, a public holiday will entitle the company to deduct a day's pay from your salary for the public holiday in question. In these circumstances, you may also be subject to disciplinary action.

If you are ill on a public holiday, the day will be treated as a day of sickness absence provided that you meet the company's normal criteria for sickness absence and:

- you notify the company at the earliest opportunity that you are sick, and
- you provide a doctor's certificate, and
- the company is satisfied your sickness is genuine.

Where your absence is accepted as sickness absence, you will receive [company sick pay/SSP] for that day according to the company's policy governing sick pay. An alternative day off in lieu will then be granted, which can be taken at a later date subject to the approval of your line manager.

Employees who have had a lengthy period of sickness absence will lose their entitlement to a day off in lieu for any public holiday which occurs after they have been off sick for 3 months (until they return to work).